LAST DAY EVERY DAY: FIGURAL THINKING FROM AUERBACH AND KRACAUER TO AGAMBEN AND BRENEZ

Last Day Every Day

Figural Thinking from Auerbach and Kracauer to Agamben and Brenez

Adrian Martin

dead letter office

BABEL Working Group

punctum books ✳ brooklyn, ny

First published in 2012 by
Dead Letter Office, BABEL Working Group
an imprint of punctum books
Brooklyn, New York
http://punctumbooks.com

The **BABEL Working Group** is a collective and
desiring-assemblage of scholar-gypsies with no leaders
or followers, no top and no bottom, and only a middle.
BABEL roams and stalks the ruins of the post-
historical university as a multiplicity, a pack, looking
for other roaming packs and multiplicities with which
to cohabit and build temporary shelters for intellectual
vagabonds. We also take in strays.

ISBN-10: 0615719465
ISBN-13: 978-0615719467

Images on Cover: Dorothy Malone and Robert Stack in
Douglas Sirk's 1958 *The Tarnished Angels* (top);
Marlene Dietrich as Lola-Lola in Josef von Sternberg's
1930 *The Blue Angel/De blaue Engel* (bottom).

Para Cristina Álvarez López

In cinema, only the *presumption* of figures exists.

~Nicole Brenez

☀ Last Day Every Day: Figural Thinking from Auerbach and Kracauer to Agamben and Brenez

Adrian Martin

Once in Melbourne, about 25 years ago, I saw Gayatri Spivak give a talk in which she had laid out, on the long table in front of her, a sequence of books, side by side. Each one was upturned and set at a certain double-page, spine sticking up. The lecture consisted of her making her way down this table, picking up each book in turn — Heidegger, Freud, Derrida — every few minutes, and seemingly extemporising on a passage that she would first read aloud. It seemed a very natural, easy, spontaneous way to give a talk even though (of course) it was completely contrived, artificial and theatrical.

I could almost re-stage Spivak's impressive trick for you, because I too am going to work my way through a number of quoted passages. I, too, will be chasing a somewhat obscure, difficult idea through a set of texts — more or less in the same order that these texts came to me, the order in which they found me. The idea is that of the *figure*, which is simultaneously a very simple and a very complex business, natural and easy as well as contrived and theatrical.

I choose to start with Paul Ricoeur, and his 1974 essay "A Philosophical Interpretation of Freud." I bought the book that it appears in, *The Philosophy of Paul Ricoeur: An Anthology of His Work*, for one dollar in a book remainder store 30 years ago and, at last, I find I have need of it. (Note to self: don't throw out anything.) In this piece, a summary of his work on Freud, Ricoeur complements the idea of what he calls *archaeology* in Freud's theory,

> the restrained archaeology of instincts and narcissism, the generalised archaeology of the superego and idols, the hyperbolic archae-ology of the war of the giants Eros and Thanatos (Ricoeur 1978, 181),

with another idea that he feels is equally necessary: *teleology*. Both ideas pose an individual subject, and what Ricoeur calls "an idea of reflective philosophy." Archaeology draws the subject backward — to origins, to drives, to primal myths — while teleology draws that subject forward.

Ricoeur is candid in relation to the Master Thinker he dares appropriate here: he admits that Freud's system rests primarily on the archaeological, because it is, in his "own rigorous terms, a regressive decomposition" that "need not propose any syn-thesis." This is why teleology in Ricoeur's sense "is not a Freudian idea but rather a philosophical notion which the reader of Freud forms at his own risk" (Ricoeur 1978, 181).

So let us take this risk with Ricoeur, to see where it draws us. In what is for me the most striking and enigmatic formulation of this essay, Ricoeur writes:

> The appropriation of a meaning constituted prior to me presupposes the movement of a subject drawn ahead of itself by a succession of "figures," each of which finds its meaning in the ones which follow it. (Ricoeur 1978, 181)

This notion of the figure is one that, Ricoeur tells us, he "attached" (this is a nice word) to, while deriving it from, Hegel's *Phenomenology of Spirit*. Teleology, he adds, is "the only law for the construction of the figures of the spirit" (Ricoeur 1978, 181). Ricoeur is trying to find a model to account for what he describes as "maturation": "man's growth out of childhood." Psychology or psychoanalysis can tell us how a person "leaves his childhood," but a more extended pathway is required: a person must become

> capable of a *certain meaningful itinerary* which has been illustrated by a certain number of cultural configurations which themselves draw their sense from their prospective arrangement (Ricoeur 1978, 181, emphasis mine).

Out of the Imaginary and into the Symbolic, then, in a sense. But Ricoeur is not offering an apology for the status quo or for tidy socialisation of the individual here, nor for what he dismisses as "simply the flattest conformism" (Ricoeur 1978, 182). "Teleology is not finality," he asserts:

> The figures in a dialectical teleology are not final causes but meanings which draw their sense from the movement of totalisation which carries them along and pushes them ahead of themselves. (Ricoeur 1978, 182)

The movement of the figures of the spirit: this is a tough Hegelian abstraction to get a grip on. But I want to focus, cinematically, on the specific kind of movement that Ricoeur proposes: a movement in stages, a kind of staggered movement, with milestones all along the way. These are the figures, these pit stops of Being (station to station), and the individual becomes, takes on, comes into, some particular stage of his personality or her destiny — except that this identity or destiny is never fixed in advance.

In a lot of cultural theory and cultural work these days, we deal with a quite different idea of movement, also cinematic in inspiration: slow or fast becomings or morphings, one thing sliding into another, always at the point of transformation, perfectly fluid, and unglued. Ricoeur's recourse to the figure as his central idea or metaphor has something stately and measured about it (that plan or path of the meaningful itinerary, marching along), and it prompts many reveries of a somewhat classical variety in my memory: the doors of consciousness that open to infinity, one after another, in the dream sequence of Alfred Hitchcock's *Spellbound* (1945); the increasingly convoluted and labyrinthine parallel worlds of Roman Polanski's horror-fantasy-thriller *The Ninth Gate* (1999), like the ascending levels in a video game; Spivak's quotation-books, one next to another, down the line of the table; the voyage of homeless old Ventura from house to house, hovel to hovel, in Pedro Costa's *Colossal Youth* (2006), whose Portuguese title literally translates as *Youth on the March*.

And a certain kind of fantastic filmic narrative, equally old-fashioned and yet entirely modern, also insists in my mind: all those tales of people who physically confront their doppelgängers, or the ghosts of their former self or future self, from Monte Hellman's *The Shooting* (1966) and Federico Fellini's version of Edgar Allen Poe in *Spirits of the Dead* (1968), through Joseph Losey's *Mr. Klein* (1976) and John Cassavetes' *Opening Night* (1977), Alain Resnais' *Love Unto Death* (1984) and Ingmar Bergman's chamber psychodrama *After the Rehearsal* (1984), to Pedro Almodóvar's generational comedy-dramas, or David Lynch's psychic splittings, or Raúl Ruiz's *Three Lives and Only One Death* (1996), or Jacques Rivette's *Story of Marie and Julien* (2003), and so on. "The marriage between the mind of a twenty year old and a violent phantom turns out to be disappointing," wrote the poet René Char, "as we ourselves are disappointing" (Char 1964, 126). Ventura too, in *Colossal Youth*, seems to be some kind of ghost, a phantom with many, many children; in fact, virtually everyone he meets he greets as his long-lost child, forever bound to him — although nothing confirms or denies this hypothesis absolutely.

But I have not exactly started at the start. Not so long ago, I spent three years translating a book: Nicole Brenez's book on the American filmmaker *Abel Ferrara* (2007). It is Brenez who, it can be very exactly and truthfully said, forged the word *figure* (and all its derivations: figurative, figurable, etc.) for contemporary European film studies, even though the word had previously been deployed by Jean-François Lyotard, Stephen Heath, David Rodowick, Dudley Andrew and others. But Brenez neither refers to nor borrows from any of these relatively contemporary uses or users of the term. She creates the term anew; she sets it ablaze and works away in the light that fire gives out for her. And after finishing, after three years of working on the translation of her lengthy text on Ferrara, I realised that this word I had rendered literally hundreds of times, *figure*, was still something of a mystery to me.

As any of you who have ever translated a complex literary work will know, translation involves a sometimes difficult and always fascinating play of identification with the text and distance from it, mastery over it and an almost constant loss of grip on it. But, in some primal sense, there has to be something you don't understand in that text to keep you in there translating it, chasing it — truth on the march.

In the word *figure*, as Brenez uses it, there is exactly what you would figure there should be in it: a notion of drawing or tracing, as in figural or plastic art, a creative shaping rather than a simple mechanical reproduction; an idea of the body, but not only the human body, because there are unhuman figures, object-figures, abstract figures, many kinds of figures; and there is a figuring out, a continual essaying or experimentation. But there is more, something more enigmatic, more powerful — more enabling for Brenez herself as a writer and analyst. In her work, quite deliberately it seems to me, Brenez never defines the concept of figure in any direct, simple, clear way. She begins her massive 1998 book *On the Figure in General and the Body in Particular* by quoting an email request she received to "define *figure* briefly in two or three words." What a red rag to a bull: her elaborate, initial answer runs to several thousand words — indeed the whole 466 pages of the book artfully elaborate, string out, her answer.

I will swiftly restate three moments of action-packed definition of the figural realm in Brenez's work. First, in one of her earliest published works, a 1990 issue of the collectively produced *Admiranda* magazine devoted to the theme of *Figuration Defiguration: Propositions*, there is a Glossary at the back devoted to "Mobile Themes and Interminable Words." (And let us not forget that such glossaries or lexicons in the contemporary French critical tradition are sometimes deliberately and slyly comic in their *ratio*, as Siegfried Kracauer would say, their pose of hyper-rationality.) In these pages concluding *Admiranda*, the word *figure* is defined thus:

> The figure invents itself as the *force* of a representation, what forever remains to be constituted, that which, in the visible, tends

to the Inexhaustible. In this sense, the figure can never be confined to Man, for it is the Unforeseeable, the Unpredictable. (Brenez 1990, 76)

The second definition comes from the same Glossary. *Figuration* is defined as — get ready for this Proustian whopper of a sentence — the

symbolic game or process aiming to establish a *fixed, evolving or unstable* correlation between the plastic, aural and narrative parameters able to elicit fundamental categories of representation (such as the visible and invisible, mimesis, reflection, appearance and disappearance, image and origin, the integral and the discontinuous, form, the intelligible, the part and the whole . . .) and other parameters — which may be the same parameters, depending on the particular type of determination effected — relating to fundamental categories of ontology (such as being and appearance, essence and apparition, being and nothingness, same and other, the immediate, the reflective, inner and outer, . . .).

This definition concludes:

All these aforementioned categories can, depending on the particular case, be reprised, invented, displaced, questioned *or destroyed*. (Brenez 1990, 75, all emphases mine)

Inside Brenez's little 1995 book on Cassavetes' *Shadows* (1959) there is yet another suggestive definitional (but not definitive) list — launched from a meditation on this single word *shadows* — concerning the principles and varieties of film figures (Brenez 1995, 65–69). First, the shadow is a representational drawing, a tracing, but displaced from realism, especially the realism of character or personhood. Such a regime of shadowy representation has Greek mythic origins: the first silhouette of a lover traced around a lover's body upon a wall, or the first drawing that filled in the figure projected by a passing horse on a blank white surface. Second, the shadow is a Shakespearean designation for the most obscure and changeable realms of character: the drives, the instincts, the reflexes or, as Brenez puts it, "devastated virtualities and phantomatic possibilities" within and around every person. Thirdly, the shadows of Cassavetes' film — "silhouettes, contours, obscurities of form" — are *studies*, works in progress, people or situations or relations constantly under construction, thus reminiscent of the earlier definition cited just above, the figure as that which "forever remains to be constituted." The figure of the shadow is, in this sense, according to Brenez, "at once whiteness and blackness, same and different, absolutely there and always without form and without limits" (Brenez 1995, 67).

The fourth kind of shadow-figure listed by Brenez here is the most curious: those phantoms or ghosts that are "tutelary figures," as she calls them. Two of the African American actors in Cassavetes' film, Hugh Hurd and Rupert Crosse, in their interrelation on-screen as characters named after themselves, "reproduce trait for trait," according to

Brenez, the real-life duo formed by the jazzmen Clifford Brown and Max Roach. Thus the film is, to her eyes and ears, "filled with a certain funereal harmonics." It is a Tomb in the generic or poetic sense (as in Mallarmé), a work of mourning and tribute, not only to two special individuals but also for a more general idea, that Brenez lyrically formulates as "a friendship with the world itself, which demands a sovereign creativity" (Brenez 1995, 68–69).

Ah ha! That business of the two black guys as tutelary figures, transforming other real figures in a poetic gesture, is exactly the clue, the hook, the echo I needed to go back into the archaeology of this term. Brenez, like Ricoeur, refers to Hegel — to his *Aesthetics* rather than his *Phenomenology of Spirit* — but she does not refer to Ricoeur. The major source for her theory of the figure would seem to be (when you dig into it) the German-born literary philologist Erich Auerbach, author of the famous *Mimesis* of 1946, and of the lesser-known but no less dazzling essay "'Figura'" written in the late 1930s and later collected in a small 1959 volume with the splendid (indeed very figural) title of *Scenes from the Drama of European Literature*. The Brenezian notion of a significant relation between two points or sets (Clifford and Max in life, Hugh and Rupert on film) — a relation that is not a mere simulation, imitation or depiction, but something more charged and inventive — is pure Auerbach . . . as I shall try, as I go along, to explain.

Actually, as it happens (and as she has proudly testified), Brenez did not directly derive nor appropriate the term *figure* from Auerbach. The filiation or transmission of ideas happened in a rather spookier way — in just the same sort of unconscious or *atmospheric* way she posits when she says in a 1997 text that Jean Louis Schefer's short 1993 piece "The Accident" (reprinted in Schefer 1999)

> could not have been written before [Jean-Luc Godard's video series] *Histoire(s) du cinéma* — whether its author had seen them or not. (Brenez 1997)

Brenez says that she hit upon the term *figura* as a guiding light for her researches somewhere in the 1980s, and was then later amazed and delighted to discover Auerbach's essay of the same name — leading, at that point, to an incorporation and reinvention of some of his specific philological notions.

What I really want to point to here is the mystery of naming — the naming of an idea. Brenez named her idea — her amorphous, mobile, interminable cluster of sensations and intuitions — as one would name a painting, or a pop song . . . or a child. A name that both sums up a perceived, already-existing essence, and opens a door to some wider, hopeful future, some yet-to-be-realised state of being. The name (the idea) has a shadow zone. It creates or conjures points, stages, stations, in space as in time. Listening in 2008 to a splendid talk by Michael Taussig on drawing and witnessing (later included in his 2011 book *I Swear I Saw This: Drawings in*

Fieldwork Notebooks, Namely My Own), I was reminded of the sometimes sacred dimension of naming, giving a name, in certain religious/spiritual traditions. "Love calls you by your name," sang Leonard Cohen. And Taussig's talk of spirits had me remembering the matter-of-fact incantation of surrealist filmmaker Nelly Kaplan, when she said: "All images are incantations: you call a spirit, and that is the spirit which appears" (Kaplan 1982, 56). Thinking of the passionate materialism of Taussig or Kaplan makes me ponder what is a perennial worry for some of us: the problem, or challenge, for non-believers to understand and use a language of the sacred or the spiritual but without religion; to approach and celebrate mystery — especially poetic mystery, or what avant-garde filmmaker Ken Jacobs calls the *mystery of personality* — but without the mystical. Figural thinking, figural work, is for me mixed up or crystallised in this challenge.

Let us plunge into the core of Auerbach on *figura*. His work is a historical endeavour: to understand and elaborate a culturally and artistically powerful, very coherent system of interpretation — in particular, interpretation of the events recorded in the Judaeo-Christian Bible — and to trace its evolution from philosophy and theology through to literature and other art forms. Auerbach's special genius was to discern this specific system, this category of thought. He sought not to celebrate, defend or revive it, merely to lay it out, step by step; and he did so magisterially in the essay "Figura," as he would for the entire drama of "the representation of reality in Western literature" in *Mimesis* — a book that has recently come back to us and our contemporary moment, thanks to (among others) Edward Said.

In Auerbach's account, figuration is a system of prophecy: how certain events or people in the Old Testament, for example, prophesise (or *prefigure*) events to come in the New Testament. But the circuit of figural steps or stages or levels does not stop there. I quote an enviably lucid passage from "Figura":

> Figural prophecy implies the interpretation of one worldly event through another; the first signifies the second, the second fulfils the first. Both remain historical events; yet both, looked at in this way, have something provisional and incomplete about them; they point to one another and both point to something in the future, something still to come, which will be the actual, real, and definitive event. This is true not only of Old Testament prefiguration, which points forward to the incarnation and the proclamation of the gospel, but also of those latter events, for they too are not the ultimate fulfilment, but themselves a promise of the end of time and the true kingdom of God. (Auerbach 1959, 58)

The end of time and the true kingdom of God: here we reach the terminal event of the Last of Days, Judgement Day, the End of the World . . . and, naturally, the titles of so many apocalyptic movie blockbusters must come to mind here.

There is one particular aspect of Auerbach's rich illustration of the concept of figuration that I want to pick out here. In *Mimesis*, he returns, as he did before and after in his career, to the case of Dante. In *Inferno*, the representation of the Beyond follows a figural logic; it is

> not to the same extent as the earthly sphere, evolution, potentiality, and provisionality, but God's design in active fulfilment. (Auerbach 1974, 189–190)

Yet it is still imperfect and incomplete, because it waits upon the supreme, ultimate fulfilment of Judgement Day. Now, what sort of characters exist, speak and bear witness in this peculiar beyond-world? Ones that do not change, that are —all at once, forever and ever — completely themselves, sealed in their identity and destiny. They are dead, phantoms of some sort, and

> the vicissitudes of their destinies have ceased; their state is definitive and immutable except that it will be affected by one single change, their ultimate recovery of their physical bodies at the Resurrection on the Last Day. (Auerbach 1974, 190)

Auerbach is in awe of the rich physical and psychological reality with which Dante is able to invest such characters. "Their own earthly lives . . . they still possess completely, through their memories, although those lives are ended" (Auerbach 1974, 191). And although they live (as Auerbach reminds us) in flaming tombs, and are "souls parted from their bodies," with only "a sort of phantom body, so that they can be seen and can communicate and suffer," nonetheless "the impression they produce is not that they are dead — though that is what they are — but alive" (Auerbach 1974, 190, 191). I would suggest to you that the characters of Dante's Beyond, as articulated by Auerbach, are profoundly cinematic creations, and it is hardly surprising that, for instance, Raúl Ruiz embraced the opportunity to fashion an avant-garde sequence of cantos from *Inferno* for television (see Martin 1993).

Now I shall draw the line connecting a circle of figures who are, again, a small circle of friends, also with an intimate relation to a "sovereign creativity" — and all touched, it seems, by the particular progressive spirits of Weimar culture. Auerbach and Walter Benjamin, as we know from the fragments of their warm correspondence that have appeared in German and English (see Barck 1992), were friends over many years. Benjamin greatly admired Auerbach's earliest major work from the late 1920s, which was precisely his first work on Dante and figural interpretation in 1929.

I would like to briefly cite a fragment by Benjamin written earlier still, in 1919-1920, unpublished in his lifetime but translated into English in Volume One of the *Selected Writings*, called "World and Time." It is a shamelessly figural contemplation, and it begins:

> In the revelation of the divine, the world —
> the theatre of history — is subjected to a
> great process of decomposition, while time —
> the life of him who represents it — is
> subjected to a great process of fulfilment.
> (Benjamin 1996, 226)

In the next two sentences, he evokes the "end of the world: the destruction and liberation of a (dramatic) representation," and the "redemption of history from the one who represents it."

This paragraph ends by wondering whether "the profoundest antithesis to 'world' is not 'time' but 'the world to come.'" Later on, a materialist inflection emerges: "My definition of politics: the fulfilment of an unimproved humanity." "The divine manifests itself" in the social — which is itself a "manifestation of spectral and demonic powers" — "only in revolutionary force." "Such manifestations," he concludes, "are to be sought not in the sphere of the social but in perception oriented toward revelation" and toward "sacred language" (Benjamin 1996, 227). These fiery motifs, as we know, never entirely left Benjamin's work.

Siegfried Kracauer, the next friend in this circle or chain, was especially fixed on these aspects of visionary thought in his 1928 essay "On the Writings of Walter Benjamin," collected in *The Mass Ornament*. "Such thinking is more akin to talmudic writings and medieval tractates," he remarked, "for like these, its manner of presentation is interpretation. Its intentions are of a theological sort" (Kracauer 2005, 259). Kracauer's terms echo, consciously or not, those of Auerbach's history of the figure.

Redemption calls, and it sings. In Kracauer's account of Benjamin, the earthly world, "*obscured and obstructed,*" must be "smash[ed] in order to reach the essentialities." Kracauer describes this world of essentialities as "ancestral," there "from the beginning" (Kracauer 2005, 261, 260). The present of "living constructs and phenomena" in Benjamin seems "jumbled like a dream, whereas once they are in a state of disintegration they become clearer" (Kracauer 2005, 262). This type of figural analysis, as practiced by Benjamin or Kracauer, thus points away from the present and simultaneously towards a primordial past and a Utopian future. (Mention of Utopia would seem to haul Ernst Bloch, too, into this Weimar circle discussion group, but I am setting consideration of him aside here, for I feel his notion of the 'spirit of hope' does not quite function, imagistically or dramatically, like an Auerbachian procession of figures: it's not at all the same hall of mirrors.)

Some time earlier, between 1922 and 1925, Kracauer wrote a short book on *The Detective Novel*. (It figures among the key references in Brenez's book on Abel Ferrara.) Kracauer chose not to publish the book in his lifetime, except for a condensed excerpt as the essay "The Hotel Lobby" in *The Mass Ornament*; the entire text appears in his collected writings in German, but has not yet been translated into English. I know it from the paperback French translation that, quite wonderfully, has a still from Hitchcock's *Vertigo* (1958) adorning its yellow-brownish cover.

In the useful introduction to this edition, co-translator Rainer Rochlitz ventures that Kracauer put the manuscript aside in 1925 because the "alliance of sociology and existential theology no longer satisfied him" (Kracauer 2001, 24); like his friend Benjamin, he had already begun moving towards a more Marxist, materialist knowledge system. Nonetheless, the theological aspects of Kracauer's *The Detective Novel* remain fascinating, and they chime in with the particular figural thinking, the resurgence or reinvention of it, prevalent in the Weimar period.

On the first page of the text (after a brief introduction predicting our current critique of globalisation, since in the international milieu of early 20th-century crime fiction, all countries are rendered uniform and alike, with only a few "particularities" to add some changeable local colour) (Kracauer 2001, 33), in a section that could be translated as "Spheres," or perhaps "Realms," Kracauer conjures the existence of two spheres which exist in a deformed or inverted mirror relation: the sphere of humans, in their earthly society, and the "superior realm," which, following Kierkegaard, Kracauer explicitly calls the "religious" sphere (Kracauer 2001, 35–36). In a logic that is well known to students of Kracauer, the ruthlessly rationalised, industrialised, bureaucratised world of contemporary society offers a pathetic, degraded reflection of the perfect world, the divine sphere: it is the inauthentic reflection of the authentic, a world without tragedy, the sublime or the ecstatic.

But what I want to insist on here is that this dual image of the two spheres is fully a figural set-up, a *dispositif*, this one in space rather than in time (see Martin 2011). The superior sphere is described overflowingly as the place of Messianic redemption: it is the place, to which you must "ascend," where "names will deliver their secret" — what a phrase, what an image, what an idea! — and

the self will be in relation with the supreme mystery that will carry it to its fullest point of existence. Speech and action, Being and form, will attain their extreme limit there; what is experienced will become real; won knowledge

will attain an absolute human value (Kracauer 2001, 35).

What's more, all this will happen in "the fullness of
time," Kracauer says, intensely juicing up a cheerily
banal, everyday phrase (Kracauer 2001, 50).

But how will we get there, to this Last Day? Even
by the end of the book, reflecting Kracauer's
anxieties (by the beginning of 1925) over its
intellectual and philosophical orientation, he shifts
the argument to one that is more congenial to our
own contemporary sensibility of the eternal
inbetween. The word *figure* appears frequently in
this early text by Kracauer. As in Benjamin's work of
the 1920s, Surrealism, too, makes an appearance, as
one sort of "communicating vessel" or transport
system back and forth between the two spheres,
human and divine. Thus the hero of detective fiction
comes to function, at his highest redeemable point,
as a figure of tension, one who "lives in the
intermediate spheres" (Kracauer 2001, 201),
between spheres, even if the ultimate kingdom, the
real kingdom, is not the one he ever manages to live
in. We start to see the logic of the French publisher's
cover image: Scottie (James Stewart) in *Vertigo* as
the Orphic anti-hero who wanders among the
shades and the shadows, between the realms of the
living and the dead (the Boileau/Narcejac novel on
which the film is based was in fact originally titled
D'entre les morts, and this team also wrote a non-
fiction study in 1964 called *Le roman policier*!).

Does figural thinking ever completely leave Kracauer's work? The very title of his last book, first published in 1969 three years after his death, *History: The Last Things Before the Last* (1995), resonates with the memory of the early writings I have cited. And there is, of course, the famous (or infamous), and certainly enigmatic, *redemption of physical reality* that underwrites his *Theory of Film* (1960), a book we are just now learning how to read or re-read.

It should be clear by this stage that Kracauer was far beyond talking of a simple valorisation, or even a strategic defamiliarisation, of the physical material world. The concept of redemption positively rings with the imagery of the world and its double, of the transformative and resurrectional power of this transformation, of some kind of figural fulfilment of our existence on earth. It takes more, after all, than just noticing the world, its mundanity as well as its wonders, to redeem it — for why would we need a camera, still or moving, to do that for us, when we can simply do it with our own eyes, inside our own lived experience? This is the poetic mystery of the world and its double, the mystery of any representational or mimetic art — an idea-talisman that Jean-Luc Godard has often returned to since the early 1980s.

Figural ideas, as far as I am aware, have not much been tried against those German filmmakers who were, in various ways and to various degrees, touched by the artistic and intellectual culture of the Weimar period. But I received a salutary shock, recently, on revisiting Josef von Sternberg's *The Blue Angel* (1930) starring Marlene Dietrich — a film I casually (in fact stupidly) remembered as a musty old canonical classic, weighed down, no doubt, by the technological difficulty, in this early talkie, of combining and synchronising image and sound recording systems. But the film, viewed through the filter of Auerbach and his circle, turns out to be, once again, extraordinary. What I once dismissed as creaky and static is in reality a purposive artistic schema: quite literally, a procession of figures, characters made over into figures (toys, puppets, statues, posters, figurines everywhere, etc.), laid out in repetitive configurations of plot and pictorial diagrams of entrapment, circularity, or itinerary-like sideways-mobile progressions. The film conjures, in all the brilliantly inventive ways Sternberg has up his sleeve, a resurrection, for Weimar cinema, of what Auerbach referred to as "the procession of prophets in the medieval theatre and in the cyclic representations of medieval sculpture" (Auerbach 1959, 52).

A key to the mysterious work of Sternberg is provided in Claude Ollier's great essay on the director, first published in 1973 and collected in Richard Roud's *Cinema: A Critical Dictionary* (1980a). Ollier is a celebrated novelist once linked, a little too casually, to the French Nouvelle Roman school of the 1950s and 1960s. As he makes clear in the introduction to his own 1980 book of film essays, the title of which can be translated as *Screen Memories*, his decade-long engagement with cinema criticism was motivated by an interest in seeing "how the viewing of films could be quite quickly linked to the work of a writer," in the questions posed similarly by both cinema and writing in this period about fiction, about the "treatment of texts and myths," and in their convergence around a common object (Ollier 1980b, 10–11).

What is this common object? Ollier spells it out at the very end of his text on Sternberg: the filmmaker's work, this "audacious, solitary and enigmatic" work, as he calls it, "is part of a centuries-old tradition concerning the relationship of the work of art to the world" (Ollier 1980a, 959). Ollier does not use the terminology of figure or figuration (although Brenez, in her 1997 survey piece "The Ultimate Journey: Remarks on Contemporary Theory," does cite him as a central inspiration for today's figural analyses), but his conception of the artwork and the world — *the world and its double*, as he himself puts it — is another fully figural spatial conception or image, replete with infernal, vampiric transactions between and across the spheres.

Sternberg abstracts the world, minutely and precisely, into "a universe in an advanced state of spatial rarefaction and confinement," and claims the right that his doubled world be "governed by laws other than those of imitation and representation, and certainly other than those of everyday causality" (Ollier 1980a, 952, 950). Once inside this world, what type of stories does Sternberg choose to tell, what sites does he recreate, with what kind of characters does he populate them? Ollier is definite on this point: everything is cliché and stereotype, deliberately and militantly so. In Sternberg's cinematic laboratory, "research is undertaken around the notion of the stereotype," in the context of "the stale and tabulated forms of that literature, theatre and iconography which is today described as 'for mass consumption'" (Ollier 1980a, 953):

> Here everything is strictly stereotyped in order to be brought as close as possible to the

most commonly admitted givens on the subject. The signs provided correspond exactly to what is expected on the occasion. (Ollier 1980a, 954)

This would, of course, be true of many films, good or bad, inspired or uninspired. But Sternberg goes further. For Sternberg, this material of 'mass ornamentation,' according to Ollier, "offers a condensation of dramatic and emotional features which have been inventoried long ago, rather like a series of events that have been already catalogued" (Ollier 1980a, 954). Likewise, characters — especially Dietrich as the *femme fatale* — function "as a model of the ephemeral, of the elusive, of the universally illusory" (Ollier 1980a, 955). They are stuck in their time and identity, unchanging (or else wildly changing, according to no naturalistic logic), and move like phantoms: like the obscured and obstructed detritus of the modern world for Benjamin, like Dante's ghostly, flaming creatures bearing witness as interpreted by Auerbach.

28 years on from *The Blue Angel*, Douglas Sirk makes, in perfect freedom, *The Tarnished Angels* (1958) at the heart of the Hollywood system. But it was a project born, in Sirk's mind, right back in the mid 1930s, when he had read the just-published novel *Pylon* by William Faulkner. *Positif* critic Jean-Loup Bourget has helpfully inventoried all the film's circular motifs, its dark, inverted carnival imagery and its Dance of Death atmosphere, in a 1972 piece aptly titled "Sirk's Apocalypse." But we must pay

urgent heed to another German genius, Rainer Werner Fassbinder, to get the full figural measure of this masterpiece by Sirk. He put it plainly, as well as comically:

> Nothing but defeats. This film is nothing but a collection of defeats. . . . In this film the camera is constantly in motion, acting like the people the film's about, as if something were actually going on. In reality, in the end they could all lie down and let themselves be buried. (Fassbinder 1992, 85)

Let's think, again, of Auerbach on Dante — and project that onto that most visible and least truly seen of movie conventions used by Sirk: the credit sequence.

In the beginning flurry of *The Tarnished Angels*, Sirk lines up his characters in their hierarchy, and especially in their infernally repeating, stereotyped selves, in the semantic and thematic places they will always dutifully occupy throughout the whole movie. In two furiously economical shots, we see first Burke (Rock Hudson) solicitously and foolishly trying to enter this world to which he is a stranger; then, intertwined, Roger (Robert Stack), in the pilot's seat, around whom everything turns. Next up is LaVerne (Dorothy Malone) as pressed-into-service spectacle, clothes and hair blown by the wind, and then Jiggs (Jack Carson), the pathetic hanger-on, the emasculated, manipulated guy in this triangle, popping up from the bottom of the film frame and barely able to hold his position in it, blowing in the wind worse than LaVerne even when she's parachuting (as she does later in the story). And finally, in an added shot after the title, the boss — the guy associated with the vulgar realities of money, time, place, news.

On the one hand, it's simple, professional narrative exposition (that's what David Bordwell might say); but, on the other, it's much more. What better than a credit sequence — with all its contractual constraints and obligations — to nail and expose a deathly world of hierarchy and erotic power-play? And all the characters, in dramatic terms, will continue to twist and turn in these positions, established (like a ritual, medieval figural procession) at the very start.

I follow up my little Weimar narrative with a comment on the historical status of figural thinking, across art, criticism and culture in general. I believe there are three ways of situating the figural — whether as a particular kind of art-making, or as a critical tool of art interpretation.

First, one can place it, as Auerbach does in the great march traced by the book *Mimesis*, as something that flowered and died within a specific historical time and place: precisely as a "scene from the drama of literature" (European or otherwise).

Second, one can see figural art, or figural thinking, as something that, beyond its historical moment, remains always latent, possible, virtual — something that rises up, in new forms, sometimes surprisingly. This is what I think happened during the Weimar period, partly because of the sparks rubbed by Auerbach's own analysis of Dante and others. It happens perhaps often, once we are attuned to seeing it: passages of Auerbach today read like striking prefigurations of the film work of Philippe Garrel, for example (see Martin 2009). And Jonathan Rosenbaum (1997) has proposed a persuasive reading of Godard's *Contempt* (1963) as the staging of a fraught, bittersweet combat between two of Auberbach's described and situated modes of storytelling, narration, and world-conjuring: the style of Homer, and the style of the Old Testament, which Rosenbaum renames, via Godard, as antiquity and modernity. "If *Contempt* has a single, overarching subject," Rosenbaum suggests, "it's the aching distance between the two styles Auerbach outlines and the two ways of perceiving the world they imply" (Rosenbaum 2004, 186). And Sirk and Sternberg, as we have seen, resumed their weighty figural styles way into the 1950s, with *The Tarnished Angels* for Sirk, and *The Saga of Anatahan* (1953) for Sternberg, a film which is for Ollier that director's supreme and most radical achievement (and remains, by the way, a film not legally available to see on DVD).

Then there is a third possibility, vigorously pursued by Bill Routt in his long text of 2000 on Brenez and the idea of figuration titled "For Criticism," a work to which I owe a lot here. For Routt, figural interpretation (which always tends, in his account and use of it, towards a positive delirium of allegorising) is absolutely fundamental, integral, inherent to the very act of criticism. Criticism is what fulfils the work of art, raises it up, redeems it — and also completes it, finishes it off, closing it down in the finality of the figural circuit as Auerbach first traced it. Or is the closure so very total, after all? Here I am reminded of Andrew Benjamin's presentation at a Melbourne conference on Spinoza in 2006, where he entered sympathetically into what he (following Walter Benjamin) described as the quality in an artwork to call out for its own naming, or rather its *nameability*: its potential or capacity to be named, and its invocation, directed at the critic or viewer, to assume this (by no means easy) task. Of course, neither of the Benjamins (Andrew or Walter) mean to say there is one, simple, flat name that we can affix to an artwork like a label, once and for all; the task assumed is more arduous, more labyrinthine than that. And it is potentially infinite, open. It certainly opens the door to a more detailed discussion of criticism, to be had at another time. For now, just remember: *love calls you by your name . . . .*

I will wrap up this scene in the drama of figuration by retelling a little parable composed by Giorgio Agamben for his book *Profanations*. Agamben, as is well-known, has long been exercised, from his own materialist-Marxist perspective, by the Messianic aspects of Walter Benjamin's work and legacy, and especially the key concept of *redemption* (see Agamben 2000). To borrow a phrase from Auerbach, Agamben's chosen mission is to grapple with, and somehow negotiate the revelation or illumination of a "veiled, eternal reality" (Auerbach 1959, 60) in Benjamin's thought and writing, without entirely being absorbed into its very particular religious meaning — to capitalise on, to grasp the illumination without buying into the specific belief system.

Agamben approaches all this indirectly, even casually, in his short *Profanations* piece "Judgement Day." This meditation pursues Agamben's notion that "there is a secret relationship between gesture and photography," specifically in this context, still photography (Agamben 2007, 24). Moreover, Agamben entertains the whimsical thought that "photography in some way captures the Last Judgement; it represents the world as it appears on the last day, the Day of Wrath" (another classic film title, by the way) (Agamben 2007, 23). Photography is the eye of eternity, the judgement of the fullness of time. But what does this eye see, what does it find, when the lens freezes the real?

Agamben offers a wonderfully contrived, perfectly allegorical example, and it is the one that adorns the jacket of the book: an image taken in Paris that is today considered "the first photograph in which a human figure appears" (Agamben 2007, 23) — "Boulevard du Temple" by Louis Daguerre (1838). Only one figure, in a street that, logically, should have looked busy and crowded with people, but that, because of the abnormally long exposure time for light to impress or imprint anything on the primitive apparatus used, is eerily empty, except for this one dark star / blobby mass of a human being in the lower left corner of the frame. Because he was inadvertently still, static, for long enough, his gesture has become immortalised in this historic photograph. But what gesture comes to stand for, emblematise, in fact replace this anonymous fellow of Paris? Not the ecstatic gestures of joy or pain, life or death, tracked by Aby Warburg (another Agamben obsession). In fact, an utterly banal gesture: the man, apparently, was getting his shoes shined.

Agamben loves this unglamorous apotheosis of a random citizen of modernity; but he also responds, passionately, to even this murky chap's call, through the photograph, to be remembered, memorialised. "Photography demands that we remember all this," says Agamben, "and photographs testify to all those lost names, like a Book of Life" — that's a very figural image, the Book of Life — "that the new angel of the apocalypse (the angel of photography) — holds in his hands at the end of all days" (Agamben 2007, 27).

That sounds like a very familiar, very classic figural fulfilment or redemption. But there is a beautiful last-moment twist in this final sentence of Agamben's, his final line, in its very last words. For after writing "at the end of all days," he immediately adds, redeeming the idea in a completely different way: "at the end of all days, that is, every day" (Agamben 2007, 27). Every day — the same ordinary, banal, yet magical and passionate sphere of the everyday that, as Siegfried Kracauer discerned in the writings of Walter Benjamin, is "now awaiting a recipient" (Agamben 2005, 264).

POSTSCRIPT, JANUARY 2012: GIVING BRENEZ THE LAST
WORD

This talk was first delivered in July 2008 at a
colloquium on Siegfried Kracauer — having been,
more or less, "written in a few minutes after several
years," as Brazilian poet Paulo de Paranagua testified
at the end of his 1966 "Manifesto for a Violent
Cinema." The proceedings of that lively colloquium
at Monash University (Australia) were, alas, never
published. When Nicole Brenez (some years later)
read the text, she disagreed with one central aspect
of my presentation. Her response, communicated
via email, went as follows:

> You are very right and enlightening about
> everything, my dear Adrian, except I don't
> feel at all that 'figure' is mysterious and
> obscure. On the contrary, each time I'm
> trying to be very clear: the analysis is about
> the process elaborated by the film to
> construct its own type of 'figure.' Polysemic
> and diversity don't mean it's not clear, let me
> explain why and how.
>   When I began to conceive my PhD (from
> 1985, *soutenu* in 1989), I hadn't read
> Auerbach's "Figura." But the structure of the
> word figure was very clear for me, I teach it in
> my classes often as the introduction, to give
> the tools to the students: it was the
> explanation of the Latin name 'Figura' in the
> dictionary *Le Gaffiot*, this wonderful old

dictionary we have for our Latin versions. I learned Latin since the Seconde at the Lycée expérimental de Sèvres, so the *Gaffiot* was weekly reading and use, it was always on my desk with the *Bailly*, the French-Old Greek dictionary — and they are still just behind me, *à portée de main*, as two pillars, even if I very rarely open them now.

Thanks to the *Gaffiot* (which I quote extensively in the introduction of my PhD), when I read Auerbach's "Figura," in its English version (which was given to me by Jean Clay, the publisher of éditions Macula — who gave it before to Yve-Alain Bois and Georges Didi-Huberman, on both of whom it had also a major influence), it was not a revelation but a wonderful confirmation, extension and historicisation. It may be that Auerbach was inspired too by an equivalent dictionary in German.

And of course in Latin, there is a whole field deriving from the seminal words *fingo*, *figuro* (verb) and *figura* (noun): *figuralis*, *figuraliter*, *figuratio*, *figurative* . . . All the terminology of the cinematic figurative studies comes from here, these *Gaffiot* pages. It's the structure, and then the methodological and theoretical house has to be built, and the house is open—meaning, it's the films themselves, in their singularity, that are enriching the method—so the more they are singular and unique, the more they will offer to the knowledge of figurality.

So, never reduce the richness of a film to a word, but enrich the notion with all the properly analysed concrete inventions.

REFERENCES

REFERENCES

Agamben, Giorgio. 2000. *Potentialities: Collected Essays in Philosophy*, ed. Daniel Heller-Roazen. New York: Stanford University Press.

Agamben, Giorgio. 2007. *Profanations*, trans. Jeff Fort. New York: Zone Books.

Auerbach, Erich. 1959. *Scenes from the Drama of European Literature*. Minneapolis: University of Minnesota Press.

Auerbach, Erich. 1974. *Mimesis: The Representation of Reality in Western Literature*. Princeton: Princeton University Press.

Barck, Karlheinz. 1992. "Walter Benjamin and Erich Auerbach: Fragments of a Correspondence." *Diacritics* 22(3-4): 81–83.

Benjamin, Walter, 1996. "The Metaphysics of Youth." In *Walter Benjamin: Selected Writings, Volume 1: 1913-1926*, eds. Marcus Bullock and Michael W. Jennings, 6–17. Cambridge, Mass.: Harvard University Press.

Boileau, Pierre & Narcejac, Thomas. 1954. *D'entre les morts*. Paris: Flammarion.

Boileau, Pierre & Narcejac, Thomas. 1964. *Le roman policier*. Paris: Presses Universitaires France [PUF].

Bourget, Jean-Loup. 1972. "Sirk's Apocalypse." In Jon Halliday and Laura Mulvey, eds., *Douglas Sirk*, 67–76. Edinburgh: Edinburgh Film Festival.

Brenez, Nicole. 1990. "Glossaire." *Admiranda* 5: 75–77.

Brenez, Nicole. 1995. *Shadows de John Cassavetes*. Paris: Nathan.

Brenez, Nicole. 1997. "The Ultimate Journey: Remarks on Contemporary Theory." In *Screening the Past* 2 [e-journal]: http://www.latrobe.edu.au/screeningthe past/reruns/brenez.html.

Brenez, Nicole. 1998. *De la figure en général et du corps en particulier. Invention figurative au cinéma*. Bruxelles: De Boeck.

Brenez, Nicole. 2007. *Abel Ferrara*. Champaign: University of Illinois Press.

Char, René. 1964. "The Journey is Done." *Yale French Studies* 31: 126.

Fassbinder, Rainer Werner. 1992. *The Anarchy of the Imagination: Interviews, Essays, Notes*, eds. Michael Töterberg and Leo A. Lensing, trans. Krishna Winston. Baltimore: Johns Hopkins University Press.

Kaplan, Nelly. 1982. "All Creation is Androgynous." In *Free Spirits: Annals of the Insurgent Imagination*, ed. Paul Buhle *et alia*, 68–72. San Francisco: City Lights.

Kracauer, Siegfried. 1960. *Theory of Film: The Redemption of Physical Reality*. Princeton: Princeton University Press.

Kracauer, Siegfried. 1995. *History: The Last Things Before the Last*, ed. Paul Oskar Kristeller. Princeton: Markus Wiener.

Kracauer, Siegfried. 2001. *Le roman policier*. Paris: Payot.

Kracauer, Siegfried. 2005. *The Mass Ornament: Weimar Essays*, trans. Thomas Y. Levin. Cambridge, Mass.: Harvard University Press.

Martin, Adrian. 1993. "The Impossible Scene: The Work of Raúl Ruiz." *Photofile*: 49–54.

Martin, Adrian. 2009. "The Long Path Back: Medievalism and Film." *Screening the Past* 26 [e-journal]: http://www.latrobe.edu.au/screeningthe past/26/early-europe/medievalism-and-film.html.

Martin, Adrian. 2011. "Turn the Page: From *Mise en scène* to *Dispositif*." *Screening the Past* 31 [e-journal]: http://www.screeningthepast.com/2011/07/turn-the-page-from-mise-en-scene-to-dispositif/.

Ollier, Claude. 1980a. "Josef von Sternberg." In Richard Roud, ed., *Cinema: A Critical Dictionary, Volume 2*, 949–60. London: Secker & Warburg.

Ollier, Claude. 1980b. *Souvenirs écran*. Paris: Cahiers du cinéma/Gallimard.

Paranagua, Paulo de. 1980. "Manifesto for a Violent Cinema." In Franklin Rosemont, ed., *Surrealism and its Popular Accomplices*, 43. San Francisco: City Lights Books.

Ricoeur, Paul. 1978. *The Philosophy of Paul Ricoeur: An Anthology of His Work*. New York: Beacon Press.

Rosenbaum, Jonathan. 2004. *Essential Cinema: On the Necessity of Film Canons*. New York: Johns Hopkins Press.

Routt, William D. 2000. "For Criticism (Parts 1 & 2)." *Screening the Past* 9 [e-journal]: http://www.latrobe.edu.au/screeningthepast/shorts/reviews/rev0300/wr1br9a.htm; http://www.latrobe.edu.au/screeningthepast/shorts/reviews/rev0300/wr2br9a.htm.

Schefer, Jean Louis. 1999. *Images mobiles*. Paris: P.O.L. Editeur.

Taussig, Michael. 2011. *I Swear I Saw This: Drawings in Fieldwork Notebooks, Namely My Own*. Chicago: University of Chicago Press.

W. dreams, like Phaedrus, of an army of thinker-friends, thinker-lovers. He dreams of a thought-army, a thought-pack, which would storm the philosophical Houses of Parliament. He dreams of Tartars from the philosophical steppes, of thought-barbarians, thought-outsiders. What distances would shine in their eyes!

~Lar Iyer

www.babelworkinggroup.org

Adrian Martin teaches in Film and Television Studies, and is Co-Director of the Research Unit in Film Culture and Theory at Monash University (Melbourne, Australia). A practicing film critic since 1979, he is the author of five previous books (*Phantasms, Once Upon a Time in America, Raúl Ruiz: sublimes obsesiones, The Mad Max Movies,* and *Qué es el cine moderno?*) with *A Secret Cinema* forthcoming from re:press in 2013, as well as several thousand articles and reviews. He is Co-Editor of the on-line film journal *LOLA* (http://www.lola journal.com/) and the book *Movie Mutations: The Changing Face of World Cinephilia* (British Film Institute, 2003).

LAST DAY

EVERY DAY

Printed in Great Britain
by Amazon.co.uk, Ltd.,
Marston Gate.